ANALYSIS OF

CONSUMERS RESPONSE ON

BRANDED FLASH MOBS:

EXPLORING APPLICABILITY OF A POTENTIAL

NEW MARKETING STRATEGY FOR EVENTS

OAXIES® PUBLISHING EVENTS RESEARCH SERIES

Ilaria Poluzzi, MSc

ANALYSIS OF

CONSUMERS RESPONSE ON

BRANDED FLASH MOBS:

EXPLORING APPLICABILITY OF A POTENTIAL

NEW MARKETING STRATEGY FOR EVENTS

OAXIES

PUBLISHING

OAXIES® PUBLISHING EVENTS RESEARCH SERIES

Ilaria Poluzzi, MSc | i.poluzzi@oaxies.com

ANALYSIS OF
CONSUMERS RESPONSE ON
BRANDED FLASH MOBS:
EXPLORING APPLICABILITY OF A POTENTIAL
NEW MARKETING STRATEGY FOR EVENTS

Published by OAXIES® LTD
Roseneath, 4 Hardwick Mount, Buxton SK17 6PP, UK
http://www.oaxies.com | info@oaxies.com

OAXIES® LTD is a company registered in England and Wales
Company Number: 10233754

OAXIES® is a trademark registered in the EU
Trademark Number: 016025595

ISBN-13: 978-1-9998205-1-0
ISBN-10: 1-99-982051-7

1st Edition, Copyright © 2018 by OAXIES® LTD

Copy Editing by Ilaria Poluzzi | i.poluzzi@oaxies.com
Cover Photo and Graphic Design by Simone Esposito | s.esposito@oaxies.com

Printed by CreateSpace, An Amazon.com Company

TABLE OF CONTENTS

LIST OF TABLES

AUTHOR

Ilaria Poluzzi, MSc

Communication Studies graduated, with a Master of Arts in Performing Arts Management at the University of Bologna, she also attained a Master of Science in Events Management at the University of Derby. Her specialisations include Marketing & Communication, Management and Hospitality. With Simone Esposito, she has founded the brand Oaxies®, a spa management start-up company.

ACKNOWLEDGEMENTS

I would like to express my gratitude to all the University of Derby (Buxton campus) team and lecturers for accompanying me in this academic path.

In particular, to my supervisor, Dr. Iride Azara, for having been always supportive, for the chats, for her encouragement and for the time she invested on me during this intensive journey.

I would like to thank my family without whom I would never have been able to achieve this goal. My parents, my sister and my grandma to love me, for have always accepted my decision and making them possible, for their infinite patience, for being my mentors and my toughest but constructive critics.

Thanks to my beautiful daughter, for her unconditional love and for being the best gift this year.

Thanks to my partner for have always being there, for the massive help and for never denying me support and trust, always standing by my side.

Thanks to my friends, near and far, for the advices and laughs in all these years.

ABSTRACT

Flash mob ads have distinguished themselves as a popular form of viral marketing in order to make some companies noticed (Grant et al., 2015). In fact, considering the augmenting aversion owned by consumers to conventional advertising, professionals have had to adopt creative strategies, such as viral marketing, to attract consumers' attention (Solomon 2003; Leskovec, Adamic & Huberman, 2007).

Despite recent studies have analysed branded flash mobs from a commercial and marketing point of view, some questions still have to be answered: which driving forces and emotions are on the heels of branded flash mobs audience? How flash mobs are currently impacting consumers response and experience? Are branded flash mobs an efficient innovative vehicle of marketing promotion?

This research elucidates qualitative study insights aimed to explore the applicability of branded flash mobs as a potential new marketing strategy for events and understand whether it is an effective innovative tool of marketing promotion.

In doing so, the researcher has chosen a qualitative orientated study based on the paradigm of Interpretivism, with an inductive approach. Adopting a comparative case study design, a netnographic research method has been deployed. The analysis of textual discourse represents a driven component of the netnographic method. By reason of this, a discourse analysis of YouTube comments on three branded flash mobs was developed, as previous studies have shown. YouTube comments, as looking through scrupulous lens, allow consumer behaviour analyses (Botha,

2014). The sampling strategy chosen by the author is purposive.

Ethnography on Internet, or Netnography, is a qualitative marketing research online that give information about the community of consumers studying contextualised data, a specialised form of ethnography adapted to the current social worlds computerised contingencies (Kozinets 2002). It is an interpretative method that allows to collect and manage data, then analyse and interpret them. According to Kozinets (2002), the analysis of textual discourse is so less prying than normal ethnography or focus groups, more natural than surveys or other quantitative methods. The research process of this method consists of three essential steps: the choice of an appropriate website and an accurate discourse (in this case, YouTube comments); data gathering; and conclusively analysis (Kozinets, 2002; Grant et al., 2015).

The analysis has shown that, in each of the three cases, consumers have perceived the branded flash mobs clearly as commercials and efficient tools of marketing, identifying the brands, expressing both appreciation toward the ad and the brand versus aversion toward the brand and the ad, which can be recognised as the two main themes common to the cases. Moreover, discourse analysis has detected the main reason behind the appreciation of the ad is a feeling of involvement, that is common in all the cases. An involvement that can lead to an intention of purchase.

In contrast with Grant and Boon (2013), viewers are not bored watching the ads, as it happens with usual commercials, but rather are willing to watch them several times. In addition to that, confirming Barnes (2006), it has been found a sensation of distrust, the feeling the flash mobs are false, not spontaneous but planned events where everything is staged. Users argue that it is all a set-up, the crowd is made up of actors and the big quantity of professionals, cameras and speakers do not convince them. The central elements must be spontaneity and fun because without significant planning to get a positive experience flash mob, the strategy fails. Firms will benefit from the power of branded flash mobs only when engaging people in this kind of event (Barnes,

2006). This study extends the body of knowledge on branded flash mob events as an efficient and effective tool of marketing promotion, illustrating motivations behind the appreciation versus aversion toward the ad and the brand.

1 INTRODUCTION

Flash mobs are not new but using them for marketing campaigns is. The concept of flash mobs rises as a meaningless act of gathering together, shifted into a protest and non- violent expression of beliefs, then briefly disappeared before making its way into the marketing world. With the current population's dependency on social media, as well as similar forms of mobile communication in daily life, unique forms of viral and guerrilla marketing, using these technologies, have become the norm over the past decade. Flash mobs are no exception.

The flash mob phenomenon can be explained using a variety of theoretical frameworks and concepts. As such, branded flash mobs have been suggested to possess a beneficial short-term profit by Guerrilla marketing theory (Prevot, 2009). They have sprout as a widespread form of viral advertising helping some companies get noticed (Grant et al., 2015).

The resistance of consumers to traditional advertising is growing and has obliged marketers to catch consumers' attention with creative strategies based on branded entertainment (Solomon, 2003) such as viral marketing (Leskovec, Adamic & Huberman, 2007).

Indeed, flash mobs present an interesting platform for research as understanding motivations and behaviours, behind these seemingly pointless spontaneous group activities and performances to attract attention, can provide some insight to how flash mobs can be active in our viral culture and whether it is a potential effective new marketing strategy.

Nevertheless, despite recent studies have analysed branded flash mobs from a commercial and marketing point of view some questions must be answered: which driving forces and emotions are on the heels of branded flash mobs participants and audience? How flash mobs are currently impacting consumers response and experience? Do branded flash mobs represent an efficient innovative vehicle of marketing promotion?

Building upon all of the above, this study primarily aims to bring the flash mob event phenomenon to the academia as are becoming a more common phenomenon. For this reason, it is binding that academics and marketers have a better cognition of them.

Endeavouring to comprehend the effectiveness of branded flash mobs as a communication tool, the objectives are:

• Introduce and explain the flash mob events as social phenomenon and as a new marketing concept used by firms;
• Analyse recent studies for comparisons and future development, to provide a clearer picture of what these events are;
• Develop a discourse analysis of branded flash mob videos on YouTube, as demonstrated by previous research where YouTube comments have been a meticulous tool through which analyse consumers opinion (Botha, 2014), to have a better perception of the current impact which flash mobs exert on consumers response and behaviour, unveiling hidden feelings behind this new phenomenon and understand whether it is an effective innovative tool of marketing promotion.

In doing so, in chapter two, with the intent of a first start for a discussion on the themes to be addressed and then investigated, the author provides a critical review of relevant recent studies on branded flash mobs, analysed as an efficient instrument of promotion, and a full description and background of the three case studies chosen.

The methodology that was deemed suitable for the research is illustrated in chapter three. Considering the research aim, a comparative case study design has been adopted and a netnographic research method, based on the assessment of textual discourse, has been deployed. A discourse analysis of YouTube comments on three branded flash mobs was developed: Tic Tac "Worst Breath in the World" ad, TNT Tv channel "Push to Add drama" ad and Lindsey Stirling "Master of Tides" video. The comparative component is used to strengthens the robustness and external validity of data with a triangulation of multiple cases (Yin, 2009; Saunders et al., 2009; Thomas, 2011; Veal, 2011; Denzin and Lincoln, 2013). A qualitative orientated study based on the paradigm of Interpretivism, with an inductive approach, has been deemed the most fitting to conduct a deep investigation of the relationship between consumers behaviours and firms, to the use of flash mobs events as a new marketing way of promoting brands.

Chapter 4 presents the findings of this study reporting the opinions and feeling of viewers on branded flash mobs. The themes resulting from the data analysis are then discussed in relation to the relevant literature.

The study extent the body of research on branded flash mob events as a new potential marketing opportunity as to drive consumers purchase and increase brand equity by assigning their brands and promoting relationship between the firm and consumers.

2 LITERATURE REVIEW

2.1 INTRODUCTION

In this chapter a critical review of relevant literature studies regarding branded flash mobs as an effective tool of promotion has been provided, analysing the impact on consumers behaviour and their experience, understanding the motivations behind the event of the branded flash mob participants.

This introductory chapter is intended to be a first start for a discussion on the themes to be addressed and then investigated.

2.2 THE CONTEXTUAL BACKGROUND

2.2.1 FLASH MOBS EVENTS AND VIRAL MARKETING

There are three major research bodies of knowledge identifiable in event studies, notably the meanings and impacts of festivals in society and culture, festival tourism, and festival management (Getz, 2010). Since hallmark and mega events almost certainly attract tourism (Getz, 2008; Hall, 1992), and the interaction between visitors and the host community create numerous interesting avenues for research, events slowly gain prominence in research and subsequently emerging as its own discipline (Getz, 2012). Event studies also see a significant proliferation of interdisciplinary research, such as business management and anthropology informed studies. Many destinations, many governments utilise festivals and events to meet civic needs and objectives for the local people and diversifying its tourism product, offerings to attract a wider variety of visitors (Richards & Palmer, 2010). The uses of events are also said used to combat social problems, creating social cohesiveness, reaching social change, addressing anti-social behaviour (Arcodia & Whitford, 2006; Deery & Jago, 2010; Picard & Robinson, 2006; Sharpe, 2008).

The recent integration and popularity of mobile devices, mobile phones, SMS and social networks have further helped the formation of groups (Grainge, 2011). Marketing managers are interested in public opinion in matter of groups and associations on the Internet (Plangger, 2012; Kietzmann et al., 2012). In fact, there has been a revolution by social media in the way dialogue occurs by allowing conversations (Kietzmann et al., 2011). This means companies and public figures can communicate and interact with people on a deeper profound level, but also that there is a communication and interaction of people with organisations as well as content providers, with their competitors, and more importantly, between each other (Parent et al., 2011). Most often, the content becomes viral and diffuse into a gradually increasing amount of public. Content creators are served with an easy and economic access to a potential audience of millions by social media channels (Mills, 2012). Marketers are attracted to diffuse the organisation message online and often the content generated by companies becomes viral through different media. Therefore, managers are eager to comprehend the motivations of posted messages or different content about their organisations that can drive significant audience through social media networks becoming viral (Bortha and Mills, 2012).

New and unexpected group activities have been brought by this integration and one of them is the 'flash mob'. They can be delineated as groups of connected persons who unexpectedly meet, perform a particular but harmless act, then spread right away (Grainge, 2011). These collective activities, improvised and organised via websites and mobile phones, aim to captivate the attention or make a public statement. Flash mobs create tangible networks, being the novel expression of the technological connectivity that generates aggregations and concerted behaviours (Grainge, 2011).

Between the end of the 1990s and the beginning of the 2000s, thanks to the popularity of the messages; facilitators of fast, decentralised and one-to-many communication; the creation of flash mobs is formed, quickly becoming the symbol of connectivity mobile in 2003, leading to a series of stunts in various cities such as New York, Berlin and London, which took on the status of performance art. Judith A. Nicholson states that "flash mobbing has crossed the boundaries between spectacle, activism, experiment and prank" (2005).

They have the potential to unleash very powerful messages. This is perhaps best explained by Schmitt (1999), who coined the term 'experiential marketing', after the experience economy (Pine & Gilmore, 1999), and refers to it as the migration of product-based marketing from highlighting benefits to the consumers to a more holistic approach that enables the consumers to experience the product using their own senses. In other words, consumers are left to judge on their own the quality of the product (usually an event product), and the commercial outcomes include branding initiatives and future purchase intention. Unlike product-based marketing, but very similar to service marketing, experiential products, such as an event, put their brands and products at risk of failure, and recovery is often challenging (Kotler & Armstrong, 2012).

Branded flash mobs have recently become a widespread form of viral advertising, helping some companies get noticed (Grant et al., 2015).

Indeed, with increasing consumer endurance to classical forms of advertising, more and more marketing experts have turned to creative strategies and rely on branded entertainment to attract consumers' attention (Solomon 2003), including viral marketing (Leskovec, Adamic & Huberman, 2007)

The definition of viral marketing is "eWOM" that means "electronic word of mouth" or "word of mouse", for which a marketing message of any kind; a brand or a product, linked to a company, is diffused massively, mainly via social media (Kaplan

& Haenlein, 2011). Also, viral marketing is about strategies that allow a simpler, faster and more cost- effective spread of messages, creating the chance of huge self-replication of marketing messages (Welker, 2002 in Golan & Zaidner, 2008). Surely, one of the crucial trends in today's marketing is that (Cruz and Fill 2008, Ferguson 2008) it stimulates consumers to transmit products and services, developed by the company, or audio, written information and video to others online (Kotler, 2015). However, as consumers are daily assaulted by a huge number of online content, firms are compelled to utilise the more creative strategies they can to get viral their videos (Cruz and Fill 2008, Ferguson 2008).

Another form of word of mouth highlighted by some marketers is buzz marketing which stands for the generation of excitement, creation of advertising and transmission of new brand relevant information via unexpected or even outrageous means. Users, advertisers and consumers can generate content and upload ads or videos to websites like YouTube, Vimeo, etc. to then be shared by a massive number of people. Being profitable, online videos can allow marketers to have more freedom with them. Unlike popular opinion, products should not be offensive or angular to generate rumours. On the contrary of media and advertising which are not always dispensable, companies can help to this purpose in provoking buzz. Both viral marketing and buzz try to enter the market to show a brand and its characteristics worthy of note. Some believe that these influences are driven less by the rules of sale and more by the rules of entertainment. All in all, any viral or buzzing campaign success depends on consumers' willingness to talk to other consumers (Kotler, 2015).

Being a type of content marketing, online branded flash mob ads can improve the experience of consumer, giving on pleasure a positive influence (Grant, Bal & Parent, 2012), high consumer interest and exposure to the brand (Ay, Aytekin and Nardali, 2010), driving consumers' purchase (Huang et al., 2012) and the acquisition of new customers results more targeted (Tsimonis & Dimitriadis, 2014). Branded flash mobs are an aid to firms in developing brand identity, with positioning, image changes and brand relationship development strategies (Freund, 2013).

2.2.2 FLASH MOBS

In the Oxford English Dictionary, the term flash mob appeared in 2004, with the definition of a popular meeting of absolute strangers, organised via the Internet or mobile phone, which performs a useless act and then separate again. They are organised events within a definite space, involving a mass of people or just a few, who could be or not related to the reason for the meeting and know or not each other before the flash mob (Zeitz et al., 2009). The definition given by academics such as Goldstein (2003) and Salmond (2010) is that of a temporary, semi-spontaneous community, formed in a public space to present a performance.

A flash mob is widely understood to be a sudden gathering of persons to do a particular action and then disperse just as quickly as the group reunited (Barnes, 2006). The success of the flash mob relies on media exposure and social media, by means of sharing and hit counts (Gore, 2010; Kiltz, 2011), as opposed to the reliance of actual staging in determining success in live events, as experienced by spectators live or through broadcast (Grant, 2016).

As a rule, flash mobs begin with an e-mail, announcing date, time and a series of instructions for the event, which is then forwarded by recipients to others, thus forming a collective group that is the virtual potential of mob. Usually, flash mobs are lasting approximately ten minutes. The participants arrive at the determined location, perform their action and separate (Wasik, 2006).

Bill Wasik, cultural critic and senior editor of Harper's Magazine, is believed to be the creator of the first flash mob, having generated the eight original flash mobs hitting the streets of New York in May 2003. The aim was to bring forth a social experiment that would condemn the "New York hipsters" nonconformist attitude revealing the current of commonality within the "hipster" community. Between 7:27 pm and 7:34 pm on 3rd June, about 200 people were gathered in the carpet department of Macy's department store, in Manhattan, New York, for the inaugural event. The sales clerk was alerted upon arrival: they were all living in a commune and were looking for a "love rug". For a 10-minute break, they did nothing except confusing the sales clerk, then the crowd disseminated on its own, thus ending what we now call flash mob (Grant, 2016). This was the first of Wasik flash mob series for what he called MOB Project (Nicholson, 2005). Nine years later, the use of this new form and method of execution has grown exponentially. This new type of performance art seems now fitting to all kinds of public performances, that includes pillow fights, freezes, dances and even political protests.

The very essence of a flash mob, and of events in general, is to make a memorable group experience. The impact of a flash mob is the product of the involvement of the crowd in certain behaviours and the realisation of the power of the collective. Alone participants in the flash mob activity would pass unnoticed. When the flash mob is formed, a power is produced, a powerful force both internally and externally, which serves to strengthen the group's solidarity (Turner and Killian 1957). According to Adam Arvidsson, 'one of the most important and fundamental trends in contemporary consumer society is the progressive inclusion of consumers in the processes where value is produced around products and brands' (2008, p. 326).

Speaking of which, the contemporary vision of promotion is directly related to customer relationship management, comprising the notion of relational exchange (Hoppner et al., 2015; Stephen el al., 2014) that transmit shared values, commitment, reciprocity and trust (Beck et al., 2015; Harmeling et al., 2015; Samiee et al., 2015). These relationships are the basis for the co-creation of experiences, as a platform for creating value in an interactive and joint way, using the numerous points of contact between the client and the organization (Minkiewicz et al., 2014; Vargo and Lusch, 2004). Bearing in mind that customers are active participants in the creation and design of the experiences they are willing to live (Gronroos, 2008, Gronroos and Ravald, 2011), it becomes clear that promotion must be informed, if not in a co-created sense, by the relationship between the consumer and the company. For this reason, to better promote customer value, they must participate, contribute and be involved (Rawlinson & Heap, 2017).

The result of emotional and practical meetings and interactions that a customer has with a firm is the customer experience (Soudagar et al., 2012). However, these interactions, either direct or indirect, can be very personal and subjective (Gentile et al., 2007) highlighting the role, participation and involvement of customer creating the experience. People acquire goods and services as a means to satisfy sensory, emotional and hedonistic aspirations deeper (Maklan and Klaus, 2011) and so, the importance for customers is their experience in the process of acquisition, integration and distribution, to achieve their ambitions and generate value in use (Maklan and Klaus, 2011; Rawlinson & Heap, 2017). The most important thing for organisations which distinguish themselves from the competitors is the customer experience (Adobe, 2017).

Once the brand is unique and memorable, perceived in a superior way in reputation and quality to its competitors, the customer-oriented brand equity is created and divided into two dimensions: 'brand awareness level' and 'brand image level' from the point of view of consumers (Keller 1993). The brand image concerns the robustness of perceptions around a brand, while brand awareness applies to the grade of recognition of the brand and the performance of the brand recall. It is important to analyse this perspective because it proposes precise guidelines concerning marketing strategies and helps making managerial decision (Keller, 1993).

2.2.3 BRANDED FLASH MOBS

Branded flash mobs are similar to unbranded flash mobs, including singing (Opera Company of Philadelphia's "Random Act of Culture"), choreographed dancing (e.g., BMW's "Greased Lightning"), and even kissing (Lynx Attract's "Chaos on the Buses"). Between the two, the most important difference is represented by the presence of branding, which is designed to increase equity and brand awareness. Participants are sometimes brand supporters and sometimes paid artists (Grant, 2016). Branded flash mobs actually do more, especially because these live performances are usually recorded and shared online by bystanders, whether they are good or not. It follows that companies must plan, execute and commercialise flash mobs in a different way. Manufacturers must consider logistics issues, such as obtaining insurance and permits, creating the appropriate content and strategy to ensure that the brand's logic is related to flash mobs, try routines to perfection and check their quality. There is less room for mistakes, everything must be done on time and in budget (MacLeod, 2009).

In the United Kingdom, on January 16, 2009, T-Mobile generated the first branded flash mob for "Life's for Sharing" advertising: in London's Liverpool Street station, 400 people sneak into a choreographed dance staged during the rush hours of the previous day and filmed with ten hidden cameras. The performance started with the action of a single camouflaged commuter and was built to include 350 sync-performing dancers with a contemporary and classical mixture of hits before stopping, and unexpectedly vanishing, into the aggregated crowd. Spectacular in its exposition of rhythmic synchronization and improvised sociality, the advertising focuses on those moments when unsuspecting members of the audience contributed to the performance. The 'dance' has become an immediate point of television discussion and a YouTube hit (Grainge, 2011). It was shown only once on the Celebrity Big Brother television program, but it was seen more than 15 million times online as it sprouts through e-mails, social networks and blogs (Kotler, 2015). The flash mob was the first of many public events choreographed and designed by T-Mobile to stimulate social relationships in the digital era, in their nature and potential, especially those allowed by cellular technologies. The "Life's for Sharing" campaign was based on a series of live performances that made the virtual communities physically present linking them within the urban space (Grainge, 2011). This also included an ad with a mass sung by thousands of people, informed of the event via the web and texts, and following various advertisements by an aspiring musician, Josh Ward, who was trying to create a band using the internet and free texts, thanks to the mobile phone. The ongoing promotion of "Josh's band" enclosed TV ads showing Josh selecting members of the audience in different concerts around British cities and culminating in a three-minute ad with the song itself, "Come With Me", performed by 1,107 volunteer groups. The ad was previewed exactly one year after the flash mob with a clear shape of marketing.

Bhattacharya and Sen (2003) argue that by generating a greater emotional response to a product or service, consumer loyalty can enhance by the marketer, such as branded flash mob. The branded flash mobs are in fact a form of guerrilla or viral marketing campaigns, with the intent to attract the attention of a large public on the brand, at relatively low costs.

They are appointed to interact with the media and consumers creating both a surprise effect and the spread of the advertising message (Hutter & Hoffman, 2011).

T-Mobile definitely showed this trend with its ambition to connect mobile users developing an integrated media campaign with the use of television and new media that facilitate the building of a brand community. "Life's for Sharing" was centrally based on different types of mobile and screen performances, mobilised in a promotional way. According to the agency in charge, Saatchi & Saatchi, the objective of the campaign in its articulations was to "create an event that people would like to participate in and then share" (Saatchi & Saatchi, 2009).

The T-Mobile campaign illustrates the trend for which the current thinking of brands is to engage consumers as creative participants in the process of advertising and marketing. More generally, however, it evidences, in contemporary media culture, the rise of branded entertainment. Amanda Lotz, who distinguishes the post-network advertising strategies, suggests that "branded entertainment marks a fundamental shift from intrusive advertisements pushed at audiences who are engaged in other content to advertising of such merit or interest that the audience actively seeks it out" (Lotz, 2007, p. 172). The way brand's entertainment is different from traditional advertising methods is questionable. However, the fear about the efficacy of conventional commercial advertising inspired the theorization of trade on promotional alternatives, arousing the demands of more confluence between the advertising and entertainment industries (Donaton, 2004).

The multimedia environment has become more fragmented with a fugitive public in their visualisation habits, making the choices on which spot watch or jump, thanks to digital video technologies. Branded entertainment expands advertisers' involvement for the production and paternity of contents as, unlike sponsorship and product placement that lends brands to existing television and film vehicles, it involves creating content that contextualises brand images in such attractive ways that consumers will want to include them in their media streams and personalised entertainment (Spurgeon, 2008).

After the T-Mobile campaign, more than 130 branded flash mobs were produced in Asia, North and South America, Australia and Europe. Managers, marketers and publicists have discovered that flash mobs in branding can produce an interactive and intense experience for consumers while acquiring visibility online, attracting attention to the brand to enhance its recognition and visibility and recruit consumers by making the flash mob a live TV commercial (Green 2013). Although a large number of branded flash mobs have experienced millions of YouTube views, counting views as a metric does not clearly indicate the efficacy of the ad (Grant et al., 2015). Therefore, it is mandatory that academics and marketers have a better comprehension of them, as they become more and more common. The purpose of marketing managers in producing branded flash mobs is to positively influence brand equity. This relationship, however, is totally dependent on consumers' attitude toward the ad and their attitude toward the brand (Gardner 1985; Homer 1990).

2.2.4 ATTITUDE TOWARD THE AD AND THE BRAND

One of the major scholars of branded flash mobs is Grant. In his studies he broadly tried to understand the nature, the concept and motivation of branded flash mobs. In his work 'Branded Flash Mobs: Moving Toward a Deeper Understanding of Consumers' Responses to Video Advertising' (Grant et al., 2015) he assessed the viewers' attitudes towards the ad, in order to understand the consequences of branded flash mobs, by examining 2,882 YouTube comments from three viral successful flash mob ads.

He developed a typology as an archetype of the consumer attitude matrix. These archetypes can help in the evaluation of the consumer's response based on processing (cognitive versus emotive) and position (supportive versus antagonistic) to guide the marketing managers to the use of branded flash mobs in viral campaigns. The attitudes of the spectators towards the ad or the brand were as: cognitive and antagonistic ("Righteous Ronnie"), affective and supportive ("Happy Jack"), cognitive and supportive ("Up and Adam"), and affective and antagonistic ("Debbie Downer"). It was clear to him, analysing the comments of these three videos, that there was a dissimilarity in the way viewers process the branded flash mobs, the objective of the comments and the grade of support for each of these elements. With regard to the processing of branded flash mobs by the viewers, the analysis and interpretation of the textual discourse of all three videos brought out five main themes given by the grouping of different terms: general affective response, the perceived sponsoring brand, the commercial, the people in the ad, and the performance. In particular, the first identified topic was affect: the consumer response ranged from lower-order emotions (for example, excitement and pleasure) to higher-order emotions (such as distrust). Warm feelings (lower-order emotions) towards the video were expressed from some viewers, whereas others critically examined the information in the video with higher-order emotions. In addition, the study revealed the target of the audience response by identifying two main ones: first, the reaction to advertising, which in the study refers to comments on the spot, the people in it, or the performance; and secondly the reactions to the perceived brand and the terms of the closely associated brand that caused confusion about who and what was advertising. Finally, there was a difference in the degree of support of viewers to videos. Although most of the comments on the ad were positive, which is consistent with the expectation of successful viral videos, a closer look at the discourse reveals that other users have taken an antithetical position (Grant et al., 2015).

According to one of his previous studies (Grant and Boon, 2013), the more the consumers become familiar with branded flash mobs the less easily it is possible to involve them, and therefore marketers attempts to persuade fail more often. After conducting a series of focus groups asking participants to talk about their reaction to flash mob videos and their enthusiasm and interest to share them with their friends, the researchers found that consumers are not willing to watch and share them if they are not creative, they do not arouse positive emotions and if the video does not show an audience influenced by performance. This is because consumers feel aversion to companies, with less chance then to share a video if they realise the commercial reasons behind it.

In an exploratory research of 2014, Grant merged a conceptual discussion on flash mobs in a marketing context through some studies with the intent to understand the use of flash mob by marketers and, more importantly, if these can be considered an effective means of communication and persuasion. He classified flash mobs as a subsection of guerrilla marketing, and in a content analysis of branded flash mobs on YouTube, reported the production of flash mobs by 120 unique companies in more than a dozen different sectors in 26 separate countries, mainly to promote entertainment, retail and travel organisations. Furthermore, most branded flash mobs are dance shows that are generally performed in a plaza or inside a mall. Thanks to numerous in-depth interviews, he illustrated an analysis of the behaviour and motivations of the parties involved in the branded flash mob: the producers, the audience and the participants. As a result, he discovered that branded flash mobs give the producer the opportunity to strengthen relationships with consumers, with the aim and goal of increasing customer awareness and interest in the product and associated brand, involving more potential consumers in a viral way. On the other hand, the audience has the opportunity to receive affective value and during the live event, members of the public are not alerted by any involvement of the brand or branding company. Motivations for participating are recreational or community reasons. Performing during a flash mob can motivate participation, given the spontaneous and extravagant nature of the event. It follows, a link between the motivations of the stakeholders and the effectiveness of the attempts at communication and persuasion (Grant, 2016).

For instance, according to Thomas (2010), there are specific reasons why the T-Mobile Life for Sharing ad was particularly successful: first, the shots in the video ad include many images of bystanders taking pictures and films with their phones to forward on to friends. This give credibility to flash mob, as being completely unexpected, but it also shows how the message has been sent from person to person instantly. The fact that T- Mobile is a phone company only further illustrates the ideal that indeed life is for sharing. Wasik agrees that this ad had the right marketing goals in mind as it is important to maintain the surprise element without estranging your audience, or your participants (Gidman, 2009). People do not want to show up to a flash marketing event only to find out they are part of a publicity stunt. In addition, Wasik claims ads like T-Mobile are successful because they give that sense of instant togetherness, rather than as a viral marketing campaign (Gidman, 2009).

Barnes (2006) argues that every effort has to be made to keep the event spontaneous, fun and quick. By engaging in this kind of flash mob, young people can have fun, feel unique and develop a relationship with a firm they feel understands them. The central elements however, will always be spontaneity and fun. Without significant planning to make the event a positive experience, the strategy fails. A flash mob becoming conventional is no longer a flash mob as the event looks like any other. In order to succeed, flash mobs must be held intermittently, on short notice, and have the elements of fun. Only then firms will benefit from the power of these web-enabled collectives (Barnes, 2006).

Successful marketing flash mobs have to have a sufficient "shock and awe" element as well as build the positive image of one's brand (Lim, 2009). Moreover, successful campaigns are finding ways to do something in the real world that prompts people to share it in their virtual world (Burcher, 2009).

2.3 THE ADS AND THE BACKGROUND

In order to better understand the background and marketing intentions behind the three branded flash mob events case studies, a full description of them has been provided. The three case studies are: Tic Tac "Worst Breath in the World" ad, TNT Tv channel "Push to Add drama" ad and Lindsey Stirling "Master of Tides" video.

2.3.1 TIC TAC FRANCE WORST BREATH IN THE WORLD

Ferrero "La Pire Haleine du Monde" or the "Worst Breath in the World", is an advertising campaign for Tic Tac France, developed at Ogilvy & Mather in Paris, characterised by a flash mob.

Set in the French town of Rouen, where the Tic Tac owner Ferrero's factory is based, it was launched in the weekend and quickly clocked up about 500,000 views on YouTube (Campaign Live, 2018). The campaign has been also launched on Twitter, using the hashtag #lapirehaleine, which became one of the most shared videos in France, reviving local pride and Tic Tac's 'cool'.

The format video lasts 120 seconds and is the first ever fainting flash mob.

The clip starts with the sentence "A breath of polecat, hyena, jackal, fennec fox, goat or pony can do more damage than you think" and the line at the end is: "Tic Tac. The small dose of fun that refreshes".

The video shows actors who impersonate strangers who approach innocent and unaware passers-by, in particular two boys and a girl, to get directions. When the latter begin to give directions, in less than five seconds, all those nearby collapses and the entire square of Rouen faints, all shown by the big screens. Right now, the victim understands something is happening, it's just a matter of knowing what the pay-off is (Scary Ideas, 2018).

Finally, we understand that the problem is halitosis, an issue that can be easily solved with a Tic Tac (We Love Ad, 2018).

Most of the people in the skit are real citizens of the city of Rouen, including the official basketball team, while the sixty people passing in front of the Hotel de Ville are employees of the Ferrero chocolate factory in Rouen.

The "Worst Breath in the World" campaign was created at Ogilvy France, Paris, by the executive creative director Chris Garbutt. The production is by Fighting Fish with the director François Nemeta that worked with Stéphanie Loir, Camille Chipot and Anne- Laure Cottel of the Ferrero marketing team (The Inspiration Room, 2018).

The online viral ad for Tic Tac caused a big sensation online, thanks to the live flash mob show, with more than 500,000 views on YouTube. But the most significant result was the amount of free media that could get thanks to that. Apart from the shares, the likes and tweets, Huffington Post and several magazines highlighted "Tic Tac Prank" (Creative Guerrilla Marketing, 2018).

Ogilvy's strategic planner, Hadi Zabad, explained: "The simple truth is that it is always difficult to tell someone who has bad breath, but we knew that Tic Tac could do it in a way that no other mentin could, jokingly"

The Ogilvy team filmed in Rouen, France, with more than a dozen cameras, but despite meticulous planning, they were not sure yet that it would be a success: "Making a live stunt is always a challenge. You never know if it is going to work, secondly, it is all about preparation, so it takes a lot of time to get ready, and third, you never know how good it will be until you're editing" said Creative Director Baptiste Clinet. Ogilvy & Mather Paris's executive creative director Chris Garbutt said: "We are experiencing such an exciting time in advertising, when it comes to earned media and how many people take your ideas and send them, they have to go through all the confusion on YouTube and make it worth it ".

The Tic Tac campaign is therefore an example of the increasing influence of social media and viral web marketing (Hollywood Reporter, 2018).

2.3.2 HIGH QUALITY TV CHANNEL TNT, PUSH TO ADD DRAMA AD

TNT is a high-quality entertainment channel offering new series, acclaimed movies and intense real-life stories. Their slogan is "We know drama" and the promise of their brand is "TV worth talking about". In 2012, the Turner Broadcasting launched its new TNT cable channel in the Benelux, the European region including Belgium, the Netherlands and Luxembourg. Instead of telling them a story, the new American television channel have decided to provide Flemish Belgian audiences a story to tell.

To unleash the irrepressible curiosity of people, a big red button has been put on a Flemish town square. The sign on the button urged people to "push to add drama". The video begins with the phrase: "Somewhere in a small town in Belgium, in a square where nothing happens, we put a button 'push to add drama' and we waited for someone to push it." The people who dared to push it were then confronted with an intense quick sequence of dramatic and crazy events happening in front of them, all related to the series shown on TNT. At the end a large cloth opens up saying "Your Daily Dose of Drama, from 10/04 on Telenet" and then their tagline.

The campaign, launched in mid-April 2012, has received more than 29 million views on YouTube after less than a week, over 250,000 likes, over 3.8 million Facebook shares (the second most shared advertising ever, and counting), more than 120,000 tweets, over 2,500 blog posts and massive national and international media attention (Duval Guillaume, 2018).

As reported by some YouTube comments, it seems that this spot was shot in the small town of Aarschot, which is located in the Flemish province of Brabant in Flanders, with a population of about 28,000 (Web Pro News, 2018).

2.3.3 LINDSEY STIRLING MASTER OF TIDES SINGLE LAUNCH FEATURING UE BOOM SPEAKERS

The American electronic violinist, dancer, performer and composer Lindsey Stirling, is famous on the music scene for her fusion of classical violin and electronic dance music. An innovative artist, eager to share the spotlight with technology, caused a sensation for the use of 3-D projection mapping animation.

"Master of Tides" video is the third single from the album "Shatter Me" of Lindsey Stirling, which has attracted the attention of an audience of more 70 million. This is thanks to music and consumer electronics that she used to create the live show. Indeed, the successful video catches the attention to the small but powerful EU BOOM waterproof speakers.

Ultimate Ears (UE), is a Logitech brand and has made custom-made professional earphones since the 90s but wanted to enter the market for premium consumer speakers and earphones.

UE BOOM is a 360 ° speaker that produces a bold and engaging sound in all directions, with a cylindrical design, roughly the size of a water bottle, which allows you to be lifted, leaning, hooked to a backpack or, in the case of the video hanging from a tree. It is covered with acoustic skins with plasma coating, and for this reason it is resistant to water and stains.

Given its versatility, it can go anywhere, without the need for a docking station. In fact, you can connect wirelessly to other UE BOOM speakers through the app, doubling the sound and playing the same song through all the speakers, just like in the video (Yeah Stub, 2018). UE BOOM can also connect wirelessly to smartphones via Bluetooth, to allow for song change, volume adjustment, answer to phone calls up to 50 feet away and play tracks from two different devices in turn. In addition, it has a rechargeable battery lasting 15 hours, with a single charge.

Cheap Bluetooth speakers, like the $199 UE BOOM, usually work well for indoor listening, but lose performance in open areas.

This is the reason why Ultimate Ears decided to sponsor this live performance, trying to convince viewers that its speakers can overcome noise.

Raul Roa, a Los Angeles photographer who captured the performance with his unofficial video posting it on YouTube, commented: "I thought the sound quality was pretty good, it was loud and clear like the normal music playing at the American Brand. They always play music and in reality I did not notice any difference compared to the good quality that was already present".

The performance, which was shot in July 2014 and then released on YouTube in August, was performed live in a public space, at the American at Brand in Glendale, California. Fifteen UE BOOM water-resistant speakers, around a fountain, were used and strategically placed. The unconscious public went around the violinist, dressed in a tricorn hat and a pirate suit, until Stirling began to fine-tune her electronic violin. The command to send the UE BOOM speakers online, with the touch of a smartphone, was given by the hidden director nearby (News Locker, 2018).

Before becoming a combination of steampunk, nautical theatrical performances and classical music, the video starts as a modern flash mob. The audience in the video, unaware purchaser, is evidently enchanted and surprised by the energy of Stirling and Cirque Berzerk, in a whirlwind of wild music and daring dance performances (The Qh Blend, 2018).

A violent live performance of the violinist transforms a modern shopping centre into a pirate adventure on the high seas, thanks to the courageous exhibition of the artist. Included in the spontaneous musical show were flamethrowers and water projections while Captain Lindsey, brandishing his violin and with his dances, saves her ship and the crew from the mythological forces of the sea. This includes sirens, Poseidon and even the appearance of the mightiest of all sea monsters: the Kraken (Consequence of Sound, 2018).

The music video was performed by the famous dance company Cirque Berserk, known for the fanciful gothic punk performances at Burning Man, which was masterfully combined with the Stirling composition. The choreographer instead is Suze Q, who has worked with artists such as Madonna, Kanye West, Pink, Rihanna, Justin Timberlake (Consequence of Sound, 2018).

#MakeMusicSocial is the movement that the flash mob is part of and that launched the UE BOOM speaker as a product to help people make music socially and rekindle the passion to listen to music aloud, to show that the music can be shared and appreciated by those around you (LA Story, 2018).

Stirling has always wanted to give something back to the artistic communities and her reflections on the music video of "Master of Tides" sum up her overall mission as an artist: "The reason I've always wanted to do a spontaneous performance is because you get to surprise people; you get to make people, hopefully, smile that were not expecting this. And I'm looking forward to hopefully, you know, making a memorable night for someone" (The Qh Blend, 2018).

2.4 CONCLUSION AND KEY THEMES
TAKEN FORWARD

In conclusion, the critical review of the literature regarding the recent and growing decision of many firms in the commercial world to use flash mobs events as a potential marketing opportunity, which has become increasingly common, has highlighted some key issues.

The intent of branded flash mobs is to attract the attention of the brand of a large audience, at relatively low costs, to involve consumers and the media evoking the surprise effect and dissemination. For this reason, they are in fact a form of guerrilla or viral marketing campaigns (Hutter & Hoffman, 2011).

Marketers, managers and publicists have therefore realized that by creating an interactive and intense experience for consumers, involving them in a flash mob that becomes a live television spot, they can gain visibility online, attract attention to the brand and increase its recognition, involving consumers by making the flash mob a "live" television spot (Green 2013).
However, as claimed by Grant et al. (2015) the metric of millions of views on YouTube does not indicate the full effectiveness of the ad.

A better understanding of them by marketers and academics is therefore paramount as the relationship between branded flash mob and brand equity is completely mediated by the attitude of consumers towards the ad and the brand (Gardner 1985; Homer 1990).

As claimed by one of the major scholars of branded flash mobs, Grant (2014), it is possible identify two major targets of viewers' response: the reaction to the ad, that is related to comments about the commercial, plus the people participating or the performance; and then reactions to the perception of brand and the terms closely associated to the brand that can result in confusion regarding the objective of the ad.

A closer look revealed that some users were antithetical to the ad, despite the majority of positive comments (Grant et al., 2015).

If consumers are familiar with branded flash mobs it becomes harder to get them involved and therefore many attempts at persuasion of marketers fail. Also, if flash mobs are not creative, if they do not provoke positive emotions or show no interest in the public, consumers are no longer willing to watch and share them (Grant and Boon, 2013).

Barnes (2006) supports the need to keep the event spontaneous with every effort, as well as fun and fast. A conventional flash mob is no longer flash mob as such, it becomes an event like any other and to be successful it must be done intermittently, with short notice and with the presence of fun elements (Barnes, 2006).

It is then clear that, flash mobs present an interesting platform for research as there are still many questions that must be answered to understand them in an academic and commercial point of view, as a new type of event phenomenon.

In doing so, this research aims to analyse consumers response to branded flash mob and how they impact their behaviour and experience, in order to unveil hidden feelings behind branded flash mobs' participants and audience, and understand whether it is an effective innovative tool of marketing promotion.

3 RESEARCH METHODOLOGY

3.1 INTRODUCTION

This research set out to whether branded flash mobs are perceived as an effective tool of promotion and explore the consumers response to them, in order to investigate how they impact consumer behaviour and experience, unveiling hidden feelings behind this new phenomenon and understand whether it is an effective innovative tool of marketing promotion.

In doing so, the researcher has chosen a qualitative orientated study based on the paradigm of Interpretivism, with an inductive approach.

Adopting a comparative case study design, a netnographic research method has been deployed. The netnographic method is based on the analysis of textual discourse and for this reason a discourse analysis of YouTube comments on three branded flash mobs was developed.

3.2 AIM AND OBJECTIVES

Based on the gaps identified through the literary review with regards to the existing knowledge on the topic, this study then primarily aims to bring the flash mob event phenomenon to the academia because it is a relatively new social phenomenon able to meet a variety of social needs (Anderson, 2012; Gore, 2010; Tonkin, Pfeiffer, & Tourte, 2012), and for the commercial world, a potential marketing opportunity (Barnes, 2006). Given the growing importance of branded flash mobs, it is necessary that marketers and academics comprehend them better.

It follows, the research question is: How do consumers respond to branded flash mobs?

In doing so, trying to understand the effectiveness of branded flash mobs as a communication tool, the objectives are:

- First, to introduce and explain the flash mob events as social phenomenon and as a new marketing concept used by firms;
- Second, to analyse recent studies for comparisons and future development, to provide a clearer picture of what these events are;
- Third, performing a discourse analysis of branded flash mob videos on YouTube, since previous research has shown that YouTube comments are a perspicacious way to study consumer attitudes (Botha, 2014), to know more about how they are currently impacting consumers response and behaviour, unveiling hidden feelings behind this new phenomenon and understand whether it is an effective innovative tool of marketing promotion.

3.3 RESEARCH PHILOSOPHY AND ORIENTATION

This study is a qualitatively oriented study based on the paradigm of Interpretativism, which follows the philosophical positions of subjectivism for which a single truth or reality does not exist but must be interpreted in different contexts (ontology) since knowledge is socially constructed (epistemology) and subjective (axiology). Social phenomena are multiple and intersubjective realities that live in a state of continuous construction and revision in society (Crotty, 1998; Saunders et al., 2009; Veal, 2011; Creswell, 2013). Each paradigm has its own ontology (positions regarding the nature of reality), epistemology (what is recognized as acceptable knowledge) and axiology (results on the search for personal values) (Saunders et al., 2009; Veal, 2011; Denzin and Lincoln 2013; Bryman, 2015). Using the interpretative paradigm, the researcher actively involved with the study participants to create an acceptable knowledge by providing a clear picture of the social dynamics influencing the problem posed (Saunders et al., 2009; Creswell, 2013; Silverman, 2016). Those who govern the world of research methodologies are the philosophical paradigms that give different positions regarding the development and nature of knowledge (Creswell, 2013).

It follows, the choice of the appropriate methodology identifying the philosophical foundations and the research methods that allow the achievement of the research purpose, aim and objectives at best (Saunders et al., 2009; Veal, 2011; Bryman, 2015).

Since the aim of the research is the understanding of the interactions between consumers and companies, to make use of flash mobs events as a new marketing mode for the promotion of brands, the paradigm that has been considered most suitable is the interpretative one. This is in fact the most appropriate to conduct a thorough investigation on consumers and behaviours resulting from the phenomenon under consideration.

3.4 RESEARCH APPROACH

Analysing with an ethnographic method means for the researcher to adopt an inductive approach. The inductive approach is strictly related to qualitative studies, in particular to ethnography, and associated to exploratory studies, as it starts from a small inquiry to build a theory depending on phenomenon observation (Saunders, et al., 2009; Veal, 2011; Gray, 2014; Bryman, 2015).

The inductive approach allows to explore the interactive connections between those involved in the phenomenon and the social behaviour that is expressed through the events in the study, giving the participants the opportunity to give their perceptions about the phenomena, and the researcher to go further the known providing a profound understanding of the phenomenon. This gives access to the world of research participants (Saunders et al., 2009; Veal, 2011; Silverman, 2016), analysing their behaviours and perceptions in specific social contexts (Gratton and Jones, 2004; Corbin and Strauss, 2008; Denzin and Lincoln, 2013). For

47

this reason, it was considered the most appropriate for this study.

3.5 RESEARCH DESIGN

The research design is the structure that guides data collection and analysis. Because the research is of exploratory nature, the comparative case study was chosen as an empirical investigation that understand in the depth and in its true context a contemporary phenomenon, in particular when the evidence of the boundaries between phenomenon and context is not clear, bringing a new in-depth comprehension of this (Bryman, 2004; Yin, 2014).

Yin (2014) argues that case studies can offer results to those who are directly influenced by the case (stakeholders) and to others interested in the event (audience) by giving important details on certain aspects underlined in the case.

The element of comparison helps to strengthen the robustness and external validity of the data by implementing a triangulation of the cases with the related information collected (Yin, 2014; Saunders et al., 2009; Thomas, 2011; Veal, 2011; Denzin and Lincoln, 2013) In fact, adopt a comparative case study design gives the possibility to compare and contrast the perceptions and behaviours of the three different chosen videos, highlighting differences and similarities.

In particular, the author has analysed 2,121.774 comments on YouTube from three branded flash mobs ads. The ads selected for analysis were:

- Tic Tac France - Worst Breath in the World Ad;
- High Quality TV Channel TNT - Push Button to Add Drama Ad;
- Lindsey Stirling Master of Tides single launch (Shatter Me Album) featuring UE BOOM Speakers.

Every advertisement chosen for this study had a satisfactory richness of discourse (Calder, 1977) and the selection took place following certain criteria:

1. It was perceived as an advertisement;

2. There were a high number of views (as a low number of views does not provide quantity and richness of diversity in the comments);
3. High number of comments from viewers on advertising with discussions and debates;
4. Significant variation in the type of comments related to the attitude of the spectator;
5. Diverse set of opinions, with a wide range of "Like" and "Dislike" data from the video;
6. Representation of a different sector and aimed at different demographic data.

3.6 RESEARCH METHODS

Today's online advertising offers several social platforms to discuss and different levels of interactivity, interoperability and co-creation opportunities (Campbell et al., 2011). Consumers have been empowered to hide their identities behind avatars and usernames, expressing their positive or negative opinions freely, limiting the control over discussions around the brand to managers (Grant et al., 2015). Online discussions give researchers a more in-depth and exploratory look at individual consumer behaviour (Jones, 1999) and at the relationship between consumers and brands (Churchill and Iacobucci, 2009; Malhotra, 2010). If a research question is unexplored, without an idea from the researchers of a possible answer, the exploratory research projects are more suitable (Malhotra, 2010) and the one considered most appropriate for this study was netnography.

Ethnography on Internet, or Netnography, is a qualitative marketing research online that give information about the community of consumers studying contextualised data, a specialised form of ethnography adapted to the current social worlds computerised contingencies (Kozinets, 2002). It has been accepted as a form of research and widely adopted in consumer research and marketing, an interdisciplinary field applied, open to the rapid development and use of new techniques (Kozinets, 2002). This method of interpretation allows the collection and management of online data for analysis and interpretation, based mainly on the analysis of textual discourse. According to Kozinets (2002) the analysis of the textual discourse is thus, in comparison to ethnography or focus groups, less intrusive and more natural than investigations or other quantitative methods, discovering norms and values shared in online communities, and then to be classified, another intrinsic advantage of netnography. The research process is based on three steps: the choice of a suitable website and an appropriate speech (YouTube comments); data collection; and finally analysis (Kozinets, 2002; Grant et al., 2015).

3.7 SAMPLING TECHNIQUES AND LINE OF ENQUIRY

Qualitative research wants to gather rich and deep data, acquiring a privileged vision of a small sample of participants for which the sampling strategy chosen during the research process is purposive (Saunders et al., 2009; Veal, 2011; Veal and Burton, 2014; Bryman, 2015). In order to select individuals or groups to better investigate the research problem, the scholar use his judgment (Saunders et al., 2009). (Saunders et al., 2009).

In each case study the line of inquiry was focused on:
Was the branded flash mob perceived as ad?
Was the branded flash mob perceived as an effective tool of promotion? Has the branded flash mob had a positive or negative impact?
Which has been consumers reactions and behaviour on branded flash mob? Which was consumers experience about branded flash mob?

3.8 METHOD OF DATA ANALYSIS

Interpretivism is part of the theoretical stance of social constructionism world, that is shared by many type of qualitative research, including discourse analysis (Saunders et al., 2009; V eal, 2011, Denzin and Lincoln, 2013; Silverman, 2013; Bryman, 2015; Silverman, 2016). This implies that the results of the research depend on the researcher's ability to overcome the dualism of the role, which is essential in the process of data interpretation (Saunders et al., 2009; Veal, 2011, Denzin and Lincoln, 2013; Bryman, 2015; Silverman, 2016).

The author then proceeded with a discourse analysis because it lends itself with particular attention to the language of the media, as it has the important property of filling the linguistic gap when analysing media texts (Gillespie and Toynbee, 2006) and it is a qualitative method whose analytical commitment is to study discourse as text and talk in social practices thus becoming an analysis of what people do, the focus is on language (Potter, 2012, Silverman, 2013). In particular, taking into account the work of the French cultural historian and social theorist Michel Foucault "a discourse is a social construction of reality, a form of knowledge which determines what is knowable, sayable and doable in a particular historical context" (Fairclough, 2013, p. 18). This form of analysis gives more attention to the articulated discourse through various types of visual images and verbal texts than to the practices implied by specific discourses. As Rosalind Gill (1996, p. 141) says "it uses discourse to refer to all forms of talk and texts". Discourse analysis is centrally concerned with language, with discourse, discursive formations and their productivity. But, as Fran Tonkiss emphasises: "Language is viewed as the topic of research . . . Rather than gathering accounts or texts so as to gain access to people's views and attitudes, or to find out what happened at a particular event, the discourse analyst is interested in how people use language to construct their accounts of the social world" (Tonkiss, 1998, pp. 247-8). Discourse analysis is also used to understand how images construct specific views of the social world, and to paraphrase Tonkiss, "visuality is viewed as the topic of research, and the discourse analyst is interested in how images construct accounts of the social world. This type of discourse analysis therefore pays careful attention to an image itself (as well as other sorts of evidence). Since discourses are seen as socially produced rather than created by individuals, this type of discourse analysis is especially concerned with the social modality of the image site. In particular, discourse analysis explores how those specific views or accounts are constructed as real or truthful or natural through particular regimes of truth" (Rose, 2001, p. 186).

As stated before, in netnography the coding according to Kozinets (2002) includes both data analysis and the process of interpretation of them (Spiggle 1994).

As Grant et al. (2015), each individual comment with all textual information was copied into a document directly from YouTube. To facilitate the analysis and in order to have an easier understanding of the comments, the author has decided to analyse only the ones written in English language. Moreover, for the purposes of the analysis, to maintain the genuineness and veracity of the comments, bad words will be replaced by asterisks but not eliminated. These comments were then carefully prepared, codified and interpreted, using an inductive approach through which the comments were linked to the expression of themes and categories, to understand the judgments, perceptions and experiences of the audience (Minichiello et al., 1990). Following the methodology line outlined by Kozinets (2002), to investigate similarities and differences, the data belonging to each category were compared with other data of events codified as belonging to the same category.

3.9 VERIFICATION CRITERIA

Trustworthiness, authenticity and credibility are the three main criteria that address validity in qualitative studies (Cresswell and Miller, 2000; Creswell, 2004).

The adequate measures adopted to actively address those threats, that characterise the chosen methodology, are illustrated in the table below.

Criterion	Actions
Coherence	Each recognisably different interpretation is devoid of internal; contradictions and presents a unified scheme

Rigour	Recognition and adherence to the procedural standards of nethnographic research by the text;
Literacy	The text recognises and is well informed about the literature and relevant research approaches;
Groundedness	The theoretical representation is supported by data, and the relations between data and theory are clear and convincing;
Innovation	The constructs, the ideas, the structures and the narrative form provide new and creative ways to understand systems, structures, experiences or actions;
Resonance	Obtainment of a personalised and sensitising connection with the cultural phenomenon;
Verisimilitude	Achieving a credible and realistic sense of cultural and community contact;
Reflexivity	The role of the researcher is recognised by the text and is open to alternative interpretations;
Praxis	Inspiration and empowerment of social action by the text;
Intermix	The representation takes into account the interconnection of the various modalities of social interaction, online and offline, in the members' daily experiences, as well as in their representation.

Tab. 1: Netnographic Criteria

3.10 ETHICAL CONSIDERATIONS

Ethics is the standard behaviour that guides the researcher's conduct while respecting the rights of research subjects (Saunders et al., 2009, Denzin and Lincoln, 2013; Gray, 2014; Veal and Burton, 2014; Silverman, 2016).

The use for research purposes of spontaneous conversations, if collected in a place accessible to the public, is not the research on human subjects. In fact, research concerning the collection and analysis of documents or records available and already existing publicly, is exempt from research on human subjects. Much of the netnographic observational research archive is of this type (Kozinets, 2013).

The privacy expectations of some participants in this type of research are extremely misplaced. It is in fact important to acknowledge any person using a communication system publicly available on the Internet must be aware that these systems are, by their nature and definition, mechanisms for storing, transmitting and retrieving comments (Walther, 2002).

Analysing online communities or cultural communications or their archives is not research on human subjects since the researcher does not record the identity of the communicators and can legally and easily access the aforementioned. Those are important conditions that suggest, for ethical research purposes, the use of some types and uses of cultural interactions through computers can be considered as similar to the use of texts.

As Kozinets (2013, p. 142) states "The Internet is not really a place or a text, it is not either public or private. It is not even one single type of social interactions but many types. The Internet is uniquely and only the Internet."

Furthermore, a paramount duty of ethical research conduct is to get the informed consent of research participants. Yet, as Frankel and Siang (1999, p. 8) note, "the ease of anonymity and pseudonymity of Internet communications also poses logistical difficulties for implementing the informed consent process." Starting largely from traditional face-to-face methods such as ethnography, netnography makes use of cultural information that is not provided confidentially to the researcher and therefore does not officially constitute research on human subjects, the analysis of archived messages and the download of existing posts do not require consent as required only in case of interactions or interventions (Kozinets, 2002).

Finally, according to the ethics of citation or quotation, being the online pseudonyms often referable to real names, they should be treated as real names (Langer and Beckamn, 2005) also because people do care about the reputation of their pseudonyms (Kozinets, 2002).

The table below shows the actions undertook by the researcher in order to meet the ethical criteria.

Informed Consent	No informed consent was required as no interactions or interventions occurred, but the researcher used spontaneous conversations, analysed archived messages and existing posts.
Covert of Deceptive Research	NA
Debriefing	NA
Withdrawal from investigation	NA
Protection of participants	No risk of any physical, psychological or emotional harm to participants.
Observational Research	NA
Giving advice	NA
Research in public places	The researcher used existing documents and records gathered in the publicly available communication system venue on the Internet where any person is aware that these systems are, by definition, mechanism for archiving, transmission and retrieval of comments.
Confidentiality/Data protection	Netnography uses cultural information that is not given specifically, in confidence, to the researcher. • Online pseudonyms have been treated as real names as they are often traceable to real names. • Data have been stored securely, collecting only data relevant to the study undertaken.
Animal rights	NA
Environmental protection	NA

Tab. 2: Actions taken to meet the ethical criteria

3.11. CONCLUSION AND KEY THEMES TAKEN FORWARD

Considering that the purpose of the research is to understand the interactions between consumers and companies, for the use of flash mob events as a new way of marketing to promote brands, it has been deemed appropriate to choose a quality-oriented research by following the interpretative paradigm, to conduct a profound analysis on consumers and behaviours deriving from the phenomenon analysed. The approach considered adequate for the investigation is inductive as it allows the exploration of the interactive links between the stakeholders involved in the phenomenon and the social behaviour that emerges in the events.

The qualitative research method considered most appropriate for the research question asked in this study was nethnography, or ethnography on Internet, a qualitative marketing research online, based on discourse analysis, that give information about the community of consumers studying contextualised data, a specialised form of ethnography adapted to the current social worlds computerized contingencies (Kozinets 2002).

For this reason, the researcher has proceeded with a discourse analysis of comments of three branded flash mobs on the YouTube platform. In fact, because of the exploratory nature of the research, the empirical investigation studies a phenomenon in depth and in its real context, with a purposive sampling strategy and following the netnographic ethical and verification criteria outlined by Kozinets (2002).

4 ANALYSIS AND DISCUSSION

4.1 INTRODUCTION

In this chapter the author deploys a discourse analysis of the three case studies.

Each ad chosen for this study owns a decent richness of discourse (Calder, 1977) and was selected following certain criteria such as the perception of the flash mob as an advertisement, a high YouTube view count with a relatively large number of viewer comments about the advertisement, representing discussion and debate.

4.2 DISCOURSE ANALYSIS

The three case studies have been treated independently, as they were all investigated using the analytical framework and key lines emerging from the literature. Key findings are then recombined and the themes that have been identified as common discussed, as well as a reflection on those that are specific to each of the cases.

4.2.1 WORST BREATH IN THE WORLD COMMENTS DISCOURSE ANALYSIS

The overall opinion about the ad is positive, with 3.434 likes and 67 dislikes, and it can count 829.245 views.

The campaign was targeted to French market and indeed the majority of comments are from French users but the 36% of them are from different part of the world, such as Russia, United

Kingdom, USA, Italy and Arab population, which can indicate the virality of the video.

As said in chapter 3, to facilitate the analysis and in order to have an easier understanding the author has decided to analyse only English comments.
In doing so, we can identify some major thematic emerging from this ad.

The 91% of people commenting the flash mob video has liked it as an advertising campaign which indicate the flash mob has been recognised as a commercial.

"That's how I like commercials to be!!"

Moreover, users have liked the video not only appreciating it as an advertising campaign but also recognising and paying tribute to the brand. This can be seen as an indicator the flash mob has been perceived as an efficient tool of communication and promotion.

"Very nice tic tac"

or

"Just amazing...the whole activation is just amazing...very well-done Tic Tac team"

However, not all users express such positive comments.
Despite being the minority, the 9% of users expressed their aversion to the ad, which they find not remarkable or exciting.

"I really don't like creativity on this stupid commercial aim! I will never ever buy that product! "

In this case, the ad is seen as poor and useless, an inefficient tool of communication because is not helping the promotion of the product but rather is putting it in a bad light. Instead of being a useful tool of communication the ad is not communicating anything to them.

"Oh dear. When will people in advertising realise that they aren't interesting - and they have nothing interesting to say? Every day that goes by their ideas are being exposed as being truly pathetic. This is a prime example."

It is interesting to note how, although both comments present the same dislike opinion about the advertisement, there is an antithesis between them. While the first one is paying tribute to the creativity of the video, from the point of view of the second one, the ad is not creative at all but rather with little inventiveness.

In particular, some of the motivation behind the aversion to the ad is the feeling the video is false: users argue that it is all a set-up, including the passers-by considered as actors.

"Fake as f**k. Would be cool if they actually did this though"

or

"Staged"

In addition, we can find some viewers that, despite the flash mob campaign, are not impress from the brand, comparing Tic Tac to other brands.

"Tic tac is a fresh maker like Mentos. Unlike Listerine. Am I right or what?"

Or that they have not changed their mind on the product, by continuing not to buy and use it.

"Not for me, thank you. Too many calories.".

4.2.2 PUSH TO ADD DRAMA AD COMMENTS DISCOURSE ANALYSIS

For the TNT campaign the views count is 55.428.964, 406.745 likes and 6.571 dislikes. The 98,41% of comments are positive. The flash mob prank is clearly perceived as a commercial and as an efficient tool of marketing, identifying the brand.

"Push Button to Add Drama. (Advertisement TNT) Great street campaign! Not new but worth watching!"

and

"Epic Commercial!! Well Done TNT"

or

"This would have made a GREAT super bowl commercial!!!!!"

Users are nicely surprised by the action and the idea. The common feeling is the ad is great and the most beautiful one.

"Best marketing campaign ever :D" or *"Might be the best commercial ever."*

and

"Video of the best advertisement in 2012? No it's the best advertisement EVER!"

Others emphasize the concept writing in capital case, which in the internet world suggests someone is shouting.

"GREAT ACTIVATION!!!! Never gonna see again another BTL (Below-the-Line) campaign like this one. :D"

or

"This is literally the BEST COMMERCIAL EVER!!! XD" or "BEST ADVERTISEMENT CAMPAIGN EVER"

In some users' opinion, this ad should be an example of marketing for others creative commercial campaigns.

"This is how all advertising should be, that was effing EPIC =)"

or

"This is how to advertise!"

and

"Just AWESOME, I can't believe I didn't see it before O__O XD THIS IS MARKETING"

Moreover, some users highlight the fact that watching this type of ad do not bother them like the usual commercials but rather help them to be involved.

"Wouldn't it be great if more ads were awesome and less annoying?"

and

"Ahahah!!!! I wouldn't mind watching advertisements if they were all this brilliant"

Not only it does not bore them but rather, they are willing to watch the video several times.

"Seriously... this is the greatest promo ever. I've watched this so many times and I still love it. So perfect."

In addition, a user has been so involved with the ad that, although the campaign is addressed to another country, he is interested in the product anyway.

"Even though I don't speak French or Dutch I wanna watch this Tv channel :-D"

In fact, one of the motivation of the appreciation of the ad is indeed the involvement created and precisely a participant testified his amazement during the event.

"I was there and I was like whuuuuut?"

Another user expresses his regret for not having had the chance to be there.

"I wished if I was there lol"

But the majority reveal the willingness to participate.

"I wanna push the button... :-) Fantastic advertising"

Writing in capital case to emphasize the concept.

"I WANT TO PUSH THIS BUTTON!!!!"

Or, highlighting their provenance, wishing to attend a flash mob prank like that in their country.

"Wow!!!! Amazing! I'd like to push that button here in Spain XD"

and

"I really want to find this button in Russia and un-push it"

Moreover, one of the feelings found in the comments was pride: in particular, the Belgian users thanks to this campaign have rediscovered their national pride

"Makes me proud of my country"

and

"I'm proud to live in Belgium ^^"
Even though the percentage of positive comments is high, the 1,59% had a negative impression with the ad. Specifically, several discussions were found between users who did not feel involved or positively impressed by the flash mob and others that instead defend the complete success of the campaign.

User 1: "Nasty, sneaky Advertisement. I will never spend a single dime on your rubbish product, consider the name forgotten."
User 2: "Lol, how is this sneaky? It's the most in your face advertisement that has ever been created. And the most awesome."

While the first user believes the ad is misleading, claiming he would never be interested in the product because of that, the other is trying to find out the motivation behind this, supporting the thesis the advertisement is one of the best in his opinion.

Another reason, for the negative evaluation of the video is the belief it is false.

*User 1: "That is b******t. They pranced like 5 people who pressed that button in some small quiet time. So the first time they did it, the news would've spread through the whole town already, so everybody knew what the hell was going on, and no one would be fooled by it after the first attempt."*
User 2 : "I think you're missing the point of it...
User 3 : "Look how many people watched this video. Success achieved."

and

"Fake, so they did this 10 times for each 10 people there was, or the 10 people pressed that button at same time?"

or

"People's reactions are so so FAKE! People today just swallows any fake s**t on screen. ITS MAKE BELIEVE... ITS MAKE BELIEVE!!!!"

These users do not believe the reactions of protagonists are real and are not convinced by the action, claiming the all ad is false. Another user, in his answer, points out the numbers of visualisations of the video, which are really high, to support his point of view of a good commercial.

Furthermore, some perceived the flash mob as a show, not as an extemporary event, in which every move was completely planned from the beginning to the end.

"Funny... It's a great idea but it doesn't convince me completely. This Advertising recall the 'Candid Camera genre' but to be a candid camera looks way too fake (Well all CC look fake but this is quite too much fake)."

Or

User 1: "Totally staged, of course, just like all 'reality' shows." User 2 answer: "You must be a funny person"
User 1: "No its real d*****s".

4.2.3 MASTER OF TIDES VIDEO COMMENTS DISCOURSE ANALYSIS

Lindsey Stirling's "Master of Tides" video views are 71.516.552, 611.987 likes and 10.032 dislikes.

It is interesting to note that only 1% of the comments are negative, while the overwhelming majority, 99%, are positive. The flash mob was perceived as striking music video and an advertisement, so both intentions were pursued.

User 1: "Now THAT is how you advertise a product!!" User 2: "YUS XD"
User 3: "yea right =3"
User 4: "agreed"
User 5 "Amen"
User 6 "I would watch it all day."

and

"Genius commercial" or "This is one big commercial"

or

"Now this is the good kind of commercial, which people actually gets entertained"

However, not all have perceived the video as a flash mob and ad: they got involved with the entire performance but solely as a show which, in this case, indicate it was not fully understood as a commercial.

"I will always love this performance. Lindsey and the dancers are amazing"

and

"Has got to be one of the best videos on the internet!!"

and

"That was amazing, just, amazing. The music along with the choreography, the awesome lighting and water effects, plus the hilarious expressions of the crowd was just incredible."

and

"Without doubt the best video on the world" Or "The best show!"

The comments from users who have understood the commercial intent of the flash mob, are about the brand as well. Some already knew the product, others discovered it thanks to the flash mob, but both highlighted its good quality.

"Best advertisement for UE Boom: 360."

or

"UE Boom is a really good product I have mine on my desk and it's awesome!"

and

"The UE Boom is actually...very cool. And so was this video!"

and

"Lindsey Stirling = boss
UE BOOM = amazing
Lindsey Stirling + UE BOOM = So much awesome that my brains may have just blown out of the side of my head."

or

"This makes me love my UE BOOM even more. :P"

In some comments it is clear the willingness to buy the advertised products, the UE speakers and Lindsey Stirling's album, which can be an index of success of the flash mob and the marketing campaign.

"That was EPIC! The show Black Sails should beg you to have this on their show. UE Booms are awesome, I sell them at work. I listen to you on Pandora plenty of times. I really need to

invest in your albums."

and

"I now freak out whenever I see a UE Boom speaker in stores"

or

"Dang, this makes me want to go out and a UE boom. It's a wireless speaker that can play music up to 50 feet away!"

and

"I just bought a ue boom, successful advertisement; and its loud as s@#$"

or

"Wow, I wish I could have been there! Actually planning to buy a UE Boom soon :)"

Other users shared their feeling of involvement as they own UE speakers, which they appreciate, and used them to listen their favourite music artist, Lindsey Stirling, watching also her video.

"These UE BOOMS are amazing btw. My boyfriend got me one and listening to it is AMAZING. Especially to Lindsey Stirling <3"

or

"My speaker is in the video... ^_^ That's epic... #ueboom" or *"Just watched this video for the first time... and listened through my UE BOOM 2 . Then read the info. Made my heart warm =]"*

and

"lol I'm listening to this on a ue boom" and *"Funny how I*

was using my UE Boom for my phone's audio the first time I saw this."

or

"What's funny is I love her music and have a UE boom"
Despite the striking flash mob other users are not changing their mind regarding the product and its performance.

"Jeez the UE BOOMS are expensive"

or

"Cool! Too bad the audience had to listen to it on UE Booms."

In the comments we can find also a feeling of envy towards those who succeeded in being part of the performance, since they wished to participate.

"That would have been so awesome to see live. So envy everyone who was lucky enough to see it live. U rock Lindsey, I mean honestly there aren't many violin players who can play a violin and dance at the same time. That takes real talent, love ya girl u are awesome. :)"

and

"I'd love to have been there"

or

"I am so jealous of these onlookers who got such world class entertainment for free"

and

"I wish I could've been there live. That looks just AMAZINGLY THOUGHT OUT AND INCREDIBLE WOW."

and

"Aww I wish I saw this XD"

Another feeling that emerges from the comments is the sensation of a planned event and not impromptu or spontaneous like a flash mob, mainly because of the big quantity of professionals, cameras and speakers.

"Well done like always. But "spontaneous" is not a word I'd choose to describe a video with hidden cameras, boom operators, and costumed professional dancers. ;-)"

" 'Spontaneous'... (Don't get me wrong. I like her music, except for the dancing.)"

and

"I don't know if the crowd was planned or not but it is amazing to put on a show in front of a bunch of people that are recording you in their phones how you managed to keep your cool in this show I can't even imagine. Those children were amazed those people were amazed. this was beautiful."

In addition, it is worth noting a comment in which the brand's marketing effort, within the artist's performance, was not appreciated.

"Lindsey was awesome but UE Boom's attempt at marketing their product didn't make much sense...".

4.3 DISCUSSION

In the following table we can identify and compare the key findings across the three case studies, that have been treated independently.

Bearing in mind the primarily aims of this study is to bring the flash mob event phenomenon to the academia and understand how consumers respond to branded flash mobs, the line of inquiry for each case study was focused on:

Was the branded flash mob perceived as ad?
Was the branded flash mob perceived as an effective tool of promotion? Has the branded flash mob had a positive or negative impact?
Which has been consumers reactions and behaviour on branded flash mob? Which was consumers experience about branded flash mob?

TIC TAC WORST BREATH IN THE WORLD	• Appreciation toward the ad and brand; • Aversion toward the ad and the brand; • Distrust.
TNT PUSH TO ADD DRAMA	• Appreciation toward the ad and the brand; • Interest on the brand and product; • Involvement and participation; • Pride; • Distrust.
MASTER OF TIDES VIDEO FEATURING EU BOOM	• Appreciation toward the brand and products; • Involvement and participation; • Envy toward participants; • Aversion toward the brand; • Distrust.

Tab. 3: Key Findings

The analysis has shown that in each of the three cases consumers have perceived the branded flash mobs clearly as commercials and efficient tools of marketing, identifying the brands, expressing both appreciation toward the ad and the brand versus aversion toward the brand and the ad, which can be recognised as the two main themes common to the cases.

As observed by Grant et al. (2015), the target of the reaction of viewers can be recognised in two main themes: firstly, reaction to the ad, which refers to comments about the commercial, the people in it or the performance; and secondly reactions to the

perceived brand and closely associated brand terms which result-
ed in confusion regarding who and what the ad was promoting.
In particular, all the tree branded flash mob has been identified
as a commercial but in some cases the video was perceived not
as an advertisement. Taking into consideration the Tic Tac and
TNT flash mob prank some perceived them not as an extemporary event but a staging in which every move is completely
planned from the beginning to the end. The same can be found in
the Master of Tides video, where not all have perceived the video
as a flash mob but they got involved with the entire performance
solely as a show, not spontaneous, which in this case, indicate it
was not fully understood as a commercial.

Regarding the users' evaluation degree to the videos, as found
by Grant et al. in the same study of 2015, the majority of comments about the ads were positive, consistent with the virality
of the videos, appreciating the video as an advertising campaign
but also recognising and paying tribute to the brands for their
creativity. The viewers are nicely impressed by the actions, the
idea, the performances, the music to consider these flash mobs
campaign an amazing example of marketing for others creative
commercials. On the one hand, this is in contradiction to what
was found by Grant and Boon (2013) in their study, where consumers shown an aversion toward firms and were less inclined
to share a video when they realised was made for commercial
reasons. On the other hand, it confirms that consumers are not
watching flash mob videos if they are not creative, if they do not
provide a positive emotion, and if there is no audience influenced
by the performance (Grant and Boon, 2013).

Discourse analysis has detected the main reason behind the
appreciation of the ad is a feeling of involvement, that is common in all the cases.

Viewers are not bored watching the ads, as it happens with
usual commercials, but rather are willing to watch them several
times. In the TNT and Lindsey Stirling's "Master of Tides" flash
mob, linked to this feeling is the regret for not having had the

chance to be there and the willingness to participate, which can be included in the category of participation. Moreover, the desire to participate is so strong that people are feeling envy towards those who succeeded in being part of the performance.

Taking into consideration Lindsey Stirling's "Master of Tides" flash mob featuring EU speakers, this feeling is also expressed by users who share their positive experiences with the product shown, since it is used to listen to their favourite artist, Lindsey Stirling, and at the same time watching the video in question.

This involvement leads to a clear stated desire of purchasing the advertised products, which is an index of success of the marketing campaign. Indeed, Bhattacharya and Sen (2003) affirm that if marketers create a strong emotional response toward a product or service, they can grow the loyalty of consumers.

As opposed to Tic Tac flash mob campaign, where some users are not impress from the ad, or they have not changed their mind on the product and its quality, stressing their firmness not to purchase.

Another important theme emerged from the analysis is national pride. In particular, thanks to TNT flash mob campaign, Belgian users have rediscovered the love for their nation and the pleasure of being part of it.

Nevertheless, a deeper examination reveals that other viewers took a completely different position which is categorised in an aversion toward the ads and the brands.

The motivations of negative evaluations are different. Specifically, for the TNT and Tic Tac campaign, the videos are not remarkable or exciting, not creative or communicative, misleading and, for this reason, the aversion is reflected on the brand resulting in a lack of interest in the product.

However, one motivation is common to all, a sensation of distrust, the feeling flash mobs are false, not spontaneous but planned events where everything is staged.

Users argue that it is all a set-up, the crowd is made up of actors and the big quantity of professionals, cameras and speakers do not convince them.

Confirming Barnes (2006), findings have shown that once the event is creative, spontaneous, fun, quick and engaging, branded flash mobs are succeeding efficient tool of marketing, able to drive consumers' purchase intention (Huang et al., 2012). The central elements must be spontaneity and fun because without significant planning to get a positive experience flash mob, the strategy fails. Firms will benefit from the power of branded flash mobs only when engaging people in this kind of event, making them feel unique and develop a relationship with a firm they feel understands them (Barnes, 2006).

5 CONCLUSIONS AND RECOMMENDATIONS

This research aimed to analyse consumers response to brand-ed flash mob and how they impact their behaviour and experience, in order to unveil hidden feelings behind branded flash mobs participants and audience, and understand whether it is an effective innovative tool of marketing promotion. Indeed, better understanding of them by marketers and academic is mandatory as the relationship between branded flash mob and brand equity is linked to the attitude of consumers toward the ad and the brand (Gardner 1985; Homer 1990).

To do so, the researcher has chosen a qualitative orientated study based on the paradigm of Interpretivism, with an inductive approach. Adopting a comparative case study design, a netno-graphic research method has been deployed. The netnograph-ic method is based on the analysis of textual discourse and for this reason a discourse analysis of YouTube comments on three branded flash mobs was developed, as previous research has demonstrated comments are a valuable lens through which study the attitude of consumers (Botha, 2014). The sampling strategy chosen by the author is purposive. Netnography, is a qualitative marketing research online that give information about the community of consumers studying contextualised data, a specialised form of ethnography adapted to the current social worlds computerized contingencies (Kozinets 2002).

With this interpretive method the researcher collects and manages the netnographic data to then analyse and interpret them. According to Kozinets (2002), the author has found the analysis of the textual discourse unintrusive and more natural than surveys or other quantitative methods.

However, during the analysis of qualitative data the research-er has pondered on the possibility to adopt a mixed method ori-entation. Quantitative research focuses on measurements. It is about collecting and analysing objective data that are normally numeric and can be organized into statistics, it is simply a re-search that involves numbers and then deals with the quantity or measurement of some phenomena quantifying (measuring or counting) the phenomenon in numbers. It subscribes an empiri-cal approach to knowledge, more positivistic or post-positivist. For this reason, if the phenomena are measured with sufficient precision, it may be possible to make certain statements with certainty. Moreover, since this type of research tends to be con-ducted to produce results in numbers, these are objective and are not influenced by possible external factors (Crowther and Lan-caster, 2014).

The discourse analysis has shown that, in each of the three cases, consumers have perceived the branded flash mobs clear-ly as commercials and efficient tools of marketing, identifying the brands, expressing both appreciation toward the ad and the brand versus aversion toward the brand and the ad, which can be recognised as the two main themes common to the cases. More-over, discourse analysis has detected the main reason behind the appreciation of the ad is a feeling of involvement, that is com-mon in all the cases. An involvement that can lead to a positive intention of purchase.

In contrast with Grant and Boon (2013), viewers are not bored watching the ads, as it happens with usual commercials, but rath-er are willing to watch them several times. In addition to that, confirming Barnes (2006), it has been found a sensation of dis-trust, the feeling the flash mobs are false, not spontaneous but planned events where everything is staged. Users argue that it is all a set-up, the crowd is made up of actors and the big quantity of professionals, cameras and speakers do not convince them. The central elements must be spontaneity and fun because with-out significant planning to get a positive experience flash mob, the strategy fails. Firms will benefit from the power of brand-ed flash mobs only when engaging people in this kind of event

(Barnes, 2006).

Based on the key findings we can conclude that, online branded flash mob advertisements have indeed the potential to enhance consumer feeling, create a positive influence on pleasure (Grant et al., 2015), increase consumer interest and brand exposure (Ay, Aytekin & Nardali, 2010), drive consumers' purchase intention (Huang et al., 2012), and provide a more targeted acquisition of new customers (Tsimonis & Dimitriadis, 2014).

This study extends the body of knowledge on branded flash mob events as an efficient and effective tool of marketing promotion, illustrating motivations behind the appreciation versus aversion toward the ad and the brand.

Nevertheless, limitations to this research derive from the necessity of analysing only comments written in English language. In this way, the study precludes the possibility of understanding and analysing other cultures opinion.

Suggestions for academia and for future research includes the possibility of adopting a mixed method orientation to eliminate bias and objective results as well as a more extensive analysis that can illustrate the motivations and opinions, not only of a restricted geographical area, but of different ones.

BIBLIOGRAPHY

Adobe (2017). Digital Trends Report. [Online] Adobe. Available at: https://offers.adobe.com/en/ au_nz/marketing/landings/ digital_trends_2017.html [Accessed at 9 February 2018].

Anderson, J. (2012). Flash mobs revisited: Public threat or democratic freedom. Public Management, 94(2), 28.

Arcodia, C., & Whitford, M. (2006). Festival Attendance and the Development of Social Capital. Journal of Convention & Event Tourism, 8(2), 1-18.

Arvidsson, A. (2008). 'The Ethical Economy of Customer Coproduction,' Journal of Macromarketing, 28 (4): 326-338.

Ay, C., P. Aytekin, and S. Nardali (2010). "Guerilla marketing communication tools and ethical problems in guerrilla advertising," American Journal of Economics and Business Administration, 2, 280–86.

Barnes N. (2006). Mob it and sell it: Creating marketing opportunity through the replication of flash mobs. Marketing Management Journal, Spring 2006. 174-180.

Bhattacharya C.B., Sen S. (2003). Consumer–customer identification: a framework for understanding consumers relationships with companies. Journal of Marketing 67: 76–88.

Beck, J. T., Chapman, K. and Palmatier, R. W. (2015) Understanding relationship marketing and loyalty program effectiveness in global markets, Journal of International Marketing, 23(3), 1-21.

We Love Ad (2018). Available at http://www.welovead.com/en/works/details/7c1Dksvx [Accessed on 8 January 2018].

Botha, E. (2014a). "Contagious Communications: The Role of Emotion in Viral Marketing," doctoral thesis. KTH-Royal Institute of Technology, Stockholm, Sweden. (2014b). "A Means to an End: Using Political Satire to Go Viral," Public Relations Review, 40 (2), 363–74.

Bortha E, Mills AJ. (2012). Managing new media. In Online Consumer Behavior, Close AG (ed). Routledge: New York; 83–99.

Bryman, A. (2015). Social Research Methods, Oxford, Oxford University Press. Bryman, A., Lewis-Beck, M.S. & Liao, T.F. (2004). The Sage encyclopedia of social science research methods, Thousand Oaks: Sage.

Burcher, N. (2009). Viral Blog. Available at: http://www.viralblog.com/guerrilla- marketing/trafalgar-square-t-mobile- karaoke-flash-mob/ [Accessed on 8 February 2018].

Calder, B. (1977). "Focus Groups and the Nature of Qualitative Research," Journal of Marketing Research, 14 (3), 353–64.

Campaign Live (2018). Available at https://www.campaign-live.co.uk/article/tic-tac- worst-breath-earth-ogilvy-mather-paris/1126154 [Accessed on 8 February 2018].

Campbell, C., L. Pitt, M. Parent, and P. Berthon (2011). "Understanding Consumer Conversations Around Ads in a Web 2.0 World," Journal of Advertising, 40 (1), 87–102.

Churchill, G.A., and D. Iacobucci (2009). Marketing Research: Methodological Foundations, Mason, OH: Cengage

Learning.

Consequence of Sound (2018). Available at https://consequenceofsound.net/2014/09/watch-edm-violinist-lindsey-stirling-surprise- shoppers-with-a-live-performance/ [Accessed on 8 January 2018].

Creative Guerrilla Marketing (2018). Available at http://www.creativeguerrillamarketing.com/guerrilla-marketing/tic-tac-frances-worst- breath-in-the-world/ [Accessed on 8 January 2018].

Corbin, J., Strauss, A. (2008). Basics of Qualitative Research, London, SAGE. Cresswell, T. & Strohmayer, U. (2000). Urban culture, London: Arnold.

Creswell, T. (2004). Place: a short introduction, Oxford, Blackwell.

Creswell, J. (2013). Research design: qualitative, quantitative, and mixed- method approaches, Los Angeles, SAGE.

Crotty, M. (1998). The foundations of social research: meaning and perspective in the research process, London, SAGE.

Crowther, D. and Lancaster, G. (2014). Research methods. London: Routledge, Taylor & Francis Group.

Cruz, D. & Fill, C., (2008). Evaluating viral marketing: isolating the key criteria. Marketing Intelligence & Planning, 26(7), pp.743-758.

Davul Guillaume (2018). Available at http://www.duvalguillaume.com/work/tnt-we- know-drama [Accessed on 8 January 2018].

Deery, M., & Jago, L. (2010). Social impacts of events and the role of anti-social behaviour. International Journal of Event and Festival Management, 1(1), 8-28.

Denzin N., Lincoln. Y., (2013). Collecting and interpreting qualitative materials, Thousand Oaks, SAGE

Denzin, N., Lincoln, Y., (2013). The landscape of qualitative research, Los Angeles, SAGE.

Donaton, S. (2004). Madison & Vine: Why the Entertainment and Advertising Industries Must Converge to Survive. New York: McGraw-Hill.

Fairclough, N. (2013). Critical discourse analysis: the critical study of language, London: Routledge.

Ferguson, R., (2008). Word of mouth and viral marketing: taking the temperature of the hottest trends in marketing. Journal of Consumer Marketing, 25(3), pp.179-182.

Frankel, M. S. and Siang S. (1999). "Ethical and Legal Aspects of Human Subjects Research on the Internet", American Association for the Advancement of Science (AAAS).

Washington, DC, Available at: www.aaaas.org/spp/dspp/sfrl/ projects/intres/report.pdf/ [Accessed on 8 February 2018].

Freund, L. (2013). "Spontaneity for Hire: Flash Mobs Go Corporate," Wall Street Journal, May 8, Available at: http://online.wsj.com/news/articles/ SB10001424127887323798104578 453172650031706. [Accessed on 8 February 2018]

Gardner, M., (1985). The whys of a philosophical scrivener, Oxford: Oxford University Press.

Gentile, C., Spiller, N. and Noci, C. (2007). How to sustain the customer experience: an overview of experience components that co-create value with the customer. European Management Journal, 25 (5), 395-410.

Getz, D. (2008). Event tourism: Definition, evolution, and research. Tourism Management, 29(3), 403-428.

Getz, D. (2010). The nature and scope of festival research. International Journal of Event Management Research, 5(1), 1-47.

Getz, D., (2012). Event Studies: Theory, Research and Policy for Planned Events, 2nd edition, Routledge, Oxon.

Gidman, J., (2009). "A phenomenological investigation of pre-qualifying nursing, midwifery and social work students perceptions of learning from patients and clients in practice settings", University of Liverpool.

Gill, R. (1996). "Discourse analysis: practical implementation", in J.T.E. Richardson (ed.), Handbook of Qualitative Methods for Psychology and the Social Sciences. Leicester: British Psychological Society, pp. 141-56.

Gillespie, M. & Toynbee, J., (2010). Analysing media texts, New Delhi: Tata McGraw Hill.

Goldstein, L. (2003). "The Mob Rules." Time Magazine, August 10. Available at: http://www.time.com/time/magazine/article/0,9171,474547,00.html [Accessed on 8 February 2018].

Gore, G. (2010). Flash Mob Dance and the Territorialisation of Urban Movement. Anthropological Notebooks, 16(3), 125-131.

Grainge, P. (2011). A song and dance: Branded entertainment and mobile promotion. International Journal of Cultural Studies, 15(2), pp.165-180.

Grant, P.S. (2014). Understanding branded flash mobs: The nature of the concept, stakeholder motivations, and avenues for future research. Journal of Marketing Communications, 22(4), pp.349-366.

Grant, P.S., A. Bal, and M. Parent (2012). "Operatic Flash Mob: Consumer Arousal, Connectedness, and Emotion," Journal of Consumer Behaviour, 11 (3), 244–51.

Grant, P., E. Boon. (2013). "When the Persuasion Attempt Fails – An Examination of Consumers' Perception of Branded Flash Mobs." Journal of Public Affairs.

Grant, P., Botha, E. & Kietzmann, J., (2015). Branded Flash Mobs: Moving Toward a Deeper Understanding of Consumers' Responses to Video Advertising. Journal of Interactive Advertising, 15(1), pp.28-42.

Gray, D., (2014). Doing research in the real world, Los Angeles, SAGE.

Gratton, C., Jones, I., (2004). Research methods for sport studies, London: Routledge.

Green, K. (2013). "Flash Mobs: Relevant or Retired?" Engaging Guerrillas. Available at: http://engagingguerrillas.blogspot.ca/2013/03/flash-mobs-relevant-or-retired.html [Accessed on 8 February 2018].

Gronroos, C. (2008). Service logic revisited: who creates value? And who co-creates? European Business Review, 20(4), 298-314.

Gronroos, C. and Ravald, A. (2011). Service as business logic: implications for value creation and marketing. Journal of Service Management, 22(1), 5-22.

Hall, C. M. (1992). Hallmark tourist events: impacts, management, and planning. London: Belhaven.

Harmeling, C. M., Palmatier, R. W., Houston, M. B., Arnold, M. J. and Samaha, S. A. (2015) Transformational relationship events. Journal of Marketing, 79(5), 39-62.

Hollywood Reporter (2018). Available at https://www.hollywoodreporter.com/news/tic- tac-worst-breath-on-earth-viral-video-310973 [Accessed on 8 January 2018].

Homer, P.M. (1990). "The Mediating Role of Attitude Toward the Ad: Some Additional Evidence," Journal of Marketing Research, 27 (1),78–86.

Hoppner, J. J., Griffith, D. A. and White, R. C. (2015). Reciprocity in relationship marketing: a cross-cultural examination of the effects of equivalence and immediacy on relationship quality and satisfaction with performance. Journal of International Marketing, 23(4), 64-83.

Howard, J. A. (1977). Consumer behavior: Application of theory, New York: McGraw Hill.

Huang, J., S. Song, L. Zhou, and X. Liu (2012). "Attitude Toward the Viral Ad: Expanding Traditional Advertising Models to Interactive Advertising," Journal of Interactive Marketing, 27 (1), 36–46.

Hutter, K., and S. Hoffman. (2011). "Guerrilla Marketing: The Nature of the Concept and Propositions for Further Research." Asian Journal of Marketing 5: 39–54.

Jones, S. (1999). Doing Internet Research: Critical Issues and Methods for Examining the Net. Thousand Oaks, CA: Sage.

Kaplan, A. M., & Haenlein, M. (2010). Users of the world, unite! The challenges and opportunities of Social Media. Business Horizons, 53(1), 59-68.

Keller, K. (1993). "Conceptualizing, Measuring and Managing Customer- Based Brand Equity," Journal of Marketing, 57 (1), 1–22.

Kietzmann, J.H., K. Hermkens, I.P. McCarthy, and B.S. Silvestre (2011). "Social Media? Get Serious! Understanding the Functional Building Blocks of Social Media," Business Horizons, 54 (3), 241–51.

Kiltz, L. (2011). Flash Mobs: The newest threat to local governments. Public Management (December 2011), 6-9.

Kotler, P., & Armstrong, G. (2012). Principles of marketing (14th ed., Global ed. ed.). Boston: Pearson Prentice Hall.

Kotler P., Keller K. L. (2015) Marketing Management. 15th Edition. New Jersey, USA: Pearson.

Kozinets, R. (2013). Netnography. Los Angeles: Sage.

Kozinets, R. (2002). "The Field Behind the Screen: Using Netnography for Marketing Research in Online Communities," Journal of Marketing Research, 39 (1), 61–72.

Langer, R. and Beckman, S. C. (2005) "Sensitive Research Topics: Netnography Revisited", Qualitative Market Research: An International Journal, 8(2): 189-203.

LA Story (2018). Available at http://la-story.com/2014/09/ musicianperformance-artist- lindsey-stirling-stirs-it-up-at-americana-at-brand-video-makemusicsocial/ [Accessed on 8 January 2018].

Leskovec, J., Adamic, L.A. & Huberman, B.A. (2006). The dynamics of viral marketing.

Proceedings of the 7th ACM conference on Electronic commerce - EC 06.

Lim, W. (2009). Cooler Insights. Available at: http://cooler-insights.com/2009/06/are- flash-mobs-useful-in-marketing/ [Accessed on 8 February 2017].

Lotz, Amanda D. (2007). The Television Will be Revolutionized. New York: New York University Press.

MacLeod, D. (2009). "T-Mobile Dance Flashmob in London," Inspiration Room, Availabe at: http://theinspirationroom.com/daily/2009/t-mobile- dance-flashmob-in- london/ [Accessed on 8 Febraury 2018].

Maklan S. and Klaus, P. (2011). Customer experience: are we measuring the right things? International Journal of Market Research, 53 (6), 771-792.

Malhotra, N. (2010). Marketing Research: An Applied Orientation, 6th ed., Upper Saddle River, NJ: Prentice Hall.

Mills AJ. (2012). Virality in social media: the SPIN framework. Journal of Public Affairs 12(2): 162–169.

Minichiello, V., Aroni, R., Timewell, E. and Alexander, L. (1990). In-Depth Interviewing: Researching People. Hong Kong: Longman Cheshire.

Minkiewicz, J., Evans, J. and Bridson, K. (2014). How do consumers co-create their experiences? An exploration in the heritage sector. Journal of Marketing Management, 30(1-2), 30-59.

News Locker (2018). Available at http://www.newslocker. com/en-ca/region/stirling/ue-boom-speakers-and-lindsey-stirling-master-the-tides-of-technology-christian-science- monitor/view/ [Accessed on 8 January 2018].

Nicholson, Judith A. (2005) 'Mobility, New Social Intensities and the Coordinates of Digital Networks,' Fibre culture, Issue 6. http://journal.fibreculture.org/issue6/ [Accessed on 8 February 2018].

Parent M, Plangger K, Bal A. 2011. The new WTP: willingness to participate. Business Horizons 54(3): 219–229.

Picard, D., & Robinson, M. (2006). Festivals, Tourism and Social Change: Remaking Worlds. Clevedon: Channel View Publications.

Pine, B., Gilmore, J. (1998). Welcome to the experience economy, Harvard Business Review.

Plangger K. (2012). The power of popularity: how the size of a virtual community adds to firm value. Journal of Public Affairs 12(2): 145–153.

Potter, J., (2012). Discourse analysis and discursive psychology, In: Cooper, H., (ed.), APA Handbook of Research Methods in Psychology, Washington, American Psychological Association Press, Vol. 2, pp. 111-130.

Potter, J., (1996). Discourse analysis and constructionist approaches: theoretical background, In: Richardson, J., (ed.), Handbook of Qualitative Research Methods for Psychology and the Social Sciences, Leicester, British Psychological Society, pp. 125- 140.

Prevot, A. (2009). "The Effects of Guerrilla Marketing on Brand Equity," Consortium Journal of Hospitality and Tourism, 13 (2), 33–40.

Rawlinson, S. and Heap, T. (2017) International Spa Management: Principles and practice. UK: Goodfellow Publishers Limited.

Richards, G., Palmer, R., (2010). Eventful Cities: Cultural Management and Urban Revitalisation, London, Routledge

Rose, G., (2001). Visual methodologies: an introduction to interpreting visual objects, London: SAGE.

Saatchi & Saatchi (2009). 'Saatchi & Saatchi create dance mania at Liverpool St Station.' Press release, 26 January. http://www.saatchi.co.uk/news/archive [Accessed 9 February 2018].

Salmond M. (2010). The power of momentary communities: locative media and (in)formal protest. Aether: The Journal of Media Geography Spring: 90–100.

Samiee, S., Chabowski, B R. and Hult, G. T M. (2015). International relationship marketing: intellectual foundations and avenues for further research, Journal of International Marketing, 23(4), 1-21.

Saunders, M., Lewis, P., Thornhill, A. (2009). Research Methods for Business Students, (4thEd), Harlow, FT Prentic.

Scary Ideas (2018). Available at http://scaryideas.com/content/28534/Tic+Tac+Worst+Breath+in+the+World/ [Accessed on 8 January 2018].

Schmitt, B. (1999). Experiential Marketing. Journal of Marketing Management, 15(1-3), 53- 67.

Sharpe, E. K. (2008). Festivals and Social Change: Intersections of Pleasure and Politics at a Community Music Festival. Leisure Sciences, 30(3), 217-234.

Silverman, D., (2016). Qualitative research, Los Angeles, SAGE.

Solomon M. (2003). Conquering consumerspace. In Marketing Strategies for a Branded World. Amacom: New York.

Soudagar, R., Iyer, V. and Hildebrand, V. G. (2012). The Customer Experience Edge- Technology and Techniques for Delivering an Enduring Profitable and Positive Experience to Your Customer. New York: McGraw-Hill.

Spiggle, S. (1994), "Analysis and Interpretation of Qualitative Data in Consumer Research," Journal of Consumer Research, 21 (3), 491–503.

Spurgeon, Christina (2008) Advertising and New Media. London: Routledge.

Stephen, S. A., Beck, J. T. and Palmatier, R. W. (2014). The role of culture of international relationship marketing. Journal of Marketing, 78-98.

The Inspiration Room (2018). Available at http://theinspirationroom.com/daily/2012/tic-tac-for-worst-breath-in-the-world/ [Accessed on 8 January 2018].

The Qh Blend (2018). Available at https://theqhblend.wordpress.com/tag/master-of- tides/ [Accessed on 8 January 2018].

Thomas, C., (2010). The Ethical Nag. Available at: http://ethicalnag.org/2010/11/04/flash-mob/ [Accessed on 8 February 2018].

Thomas, G., (2011). How to do your case study, London, SAGE.

Tonkiss, F. (1998). "Analysing discourse", in C. Seale (ed.), Researching Society and Culture. London: Sage, pp. 245-60.

Tonkin, E., Pfeiffer, H. D., and Tourte, G. (2012). Twitter, information sharing and the London riots? Bulletin of the American Society for Information Science and Technology, 38(2), 49-57.

Tsimonis, G., and Dimitriadis S. (2014). "Brand Strategies in Social Media," Marketing Intelligence and Planning, 32 (3), 328–44.

Turner, R.H. and Killian, L.M. (1957). Collective behavior,

Englewood Cliffs, NJ: Prentice-Hall.

Vargo, S. L. and Lusch, R. F. (2004). Evolving to a new dominant logic for marketing, Journal of Marketing, 68, 1-17.

Veal, A., (2011). Research methods for leisure and tourism, Harlow, Financial Times Prentice Hall.

Veal, A., Burton, C., (2014). Research Methods for arts and event management, Harlow, Pearson Education Limited.

Walther, J. P. (2002). "Research Ethics in Internet-Enabled Research: Human Subjects Issues and methodological Myopia", Ethics and Information Technology, 4: 205-16.

Wasik, B. (2006). My Crowd: Or, Phase 5: A Report from the Inventor of the Flash Mob. Harper's Magazine 312(1870). pp. 56-66.

Web Pro News (2018). Available at https://www.webpronews.com/push-red-button-add- drama-tnt-ad/ [Accessed on 8 January 2018].

Welker (2002). in Golan, G.J. & Zaidner, L., 2008. Creative Strategies in Viral Advertising: An Application of Taylor's Six-Segment Message Strategy Wheel. Journal of Computer-Mediated Communication, 13(4), pp.959-972.

Yeah Stub (2018). Available at https://yeahstub.com/lindsey-stirling-surprises-shoppers- with-impromptu-performance-with-ue-boom/ [Accessed on 8 January 2018].

Yin, R. (2014). Case study research: design and methods, London, SAGE Zeitz, K., H. Tan, M. Grief, P.C. Couns, and Zeitz C. (2009). "Crowd Behaviour at Mass Gatherings: A Literature Review," Prehospital and Disaster Medicine, 24 (1), 32–38.

NOTES

NOTES

NOTES

NOTES

NOTES

NOTES

NOTES

www.ingramcontent.com/pod-product-compliance
Lightning Source LLC
Chambersburg PA
CBHW070929270326
41927CB00011B/2790